SEARCHLIGHT
PICTURES

# CHEVALIER

## MUSIC FROM THE MOTION PICTURE SOUNDTRACK

## FOR VIOLIN SOLO

### SCORE BY KRIS BOWERS

### FEATURING VIOLIN DUEL BY MICHAEL ABELS

ISBN 978-1-70519-853-7

Motion Picture Artwork, TM & Copyright © 2023 20th Century Studios

Visit Hal Leonard Online at
**www.halleonard.com**

World headquarters, contact:
**Hal Leonard**
7777 West Bluemound Road
Milwaukee, WI 53213
Email: info@halleonard.com

In Europe, contact:
**Hal Leonard Europe Limited**
1 Red Place
London, W1K 6PL
Email: info@halleonardeurope.com

In Australia, contact:
**Hal Leonard Australia Pty. Ltd.**
4 Lentara Court
Cheltenham, Victoria, 3192 Australia
Email: info@halleonard.com.au

# BIOGRAPHY

Joseph Bologne, Chevalier de Saint-Georges, was born Christmas Day, 1745, on the island of Guadeloupe, then a French colony, in the Caribbean Sea. His father, Georges de Bologne Saint-Georges, was a wealthy French plantation owner. His mother, known simply as Nanon, was an eighteen-year-old slave from Senegal, in West Africa on the coastline of the Atlantic Ocean. When Joseph was seven, his father sent him to Paris to be educated at a Jesuit boarding school. At thirteen he was enrolled in the renowned La Boëssière Academy, there to study music, mathematics, literature, and fencing—all essential skills for a gentleman during the Enlightenment in 18th century France.

Joseph Bologne not only excelled in these several areas, he triumphed. He became legendary as Europe's most undefeated fencer, and he was lauded as a dancer, equestrian and even as a fashion trendsetter. Soon, people were flocking to his violin concerts and he gained a reputation for pushing the instrument to its limits. He went even further as a composer, writing pioneering string quartets and helping to establish the rich symmetry and melodic hallmarks of the Baroque era. Bologne's complex and emotional compositions influenced other composers, including—many scholars suggest—his brilliant and even more-famous contemporary, Wolfgang Amadeus Mozart.

As a man of mixed race, Joseph Bologne was undeniably hampered by French law and social conventions. And while France's Enlightenment Age philosophers opposed slavery, he was well aware that the monarchy supported it. Consequently, although Bologne led a life of creative opportunity in Paris, he was never afforded the same rights as others and was subjected to limits on his freedom and, at times, to outright hatred. Even with these challenges, Bologne's remarkable virtuosity and persona allowed him to enter, however precariously, the elite circle of society enjoying wealth, power, and the outrageous excesses of the age. In 1762 Joseph Bologne even had the honor of being made an officer of the King's Guard and was dubbed Chevalier de Saint-Georges.

Despite only marginal status amongst the elite, Joseph Bologne's brilliance was such that he was hired to provide music lessons for the then-most powerful teenager in the world, the imperious Marie Antoinette, an Austrian princess who would soon become the very *last* Queen of France. In fact, it what she who spurred the French Revolution, and consequently her death by guillotine. Although only the broadest outlines of Joseph's interactions with Marie Antoinette are known, one thing was made clear: at a time when Marie Antoinette could have used her power to *aid* Bologne, she instead allowed his dreams to be crushed. In 1776, on the cusp of Joseph Bologne becoming the first person of color to head the Paris Opera—an appointment that would have been well ahead of its time—three of the Opera's leading ladies petitioned then *Queen* Marie Antoinette, declaring they could never "submit to the orders of a mulatto."

So, after being spurned for the position of heading the Paris Opera, Joseph Bologne turned from music to social change, becoming first an abolitionist and then a soldier in the French Revolution. Even in the military he proved a genius, leading France's first all-Black regiment, 1,000 men strong. Yet music was always integral to the Chevalier. He is quoted as saying, "Towards the end of my life, I was particularly devoted to my violin. Never before did I play it so well." On June 9, 1799, Joseph Bologne, Chevalier de Saint-Georges, passed away at the age of 54.

# CONTENTS

# VIOLIN CONCERTO IN G MAJOR, OP. 8, NO. 2
## I. Allegro

Violin

By JOSEPH BOLOGNE, CHEVALIER DE SAINT-GEORGES
Arranged by GARETH MURPHY

# SINFONIE LIBERTÉ
## Part 1 & 2

VIOLIN

Composed by MICHAEL ABELS
and JOSEPH BOLOGNE, CHEVALIER DE SAINT-GEORGES

# MAIN TITLE - ARRIVAL AT POLYTECHNIC

VIOLIN

By KRIS BOWERS
and JOSEPH BOLOGNE, CHEVALIER DE SAINT-GEORGES

# FENCING DUEL

By KRIS BOWERS

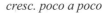

# AWARDED CHEVALIER

VIOLIN

By KRIS BOWERS

# VIOLIN DUEL

SOLO VIOLIN I & II

By MICHAEL ABELS
and WOLFGANG AMADEUS MOZART

**Allegretto**

**Rubato** ... **Allegro aperto**

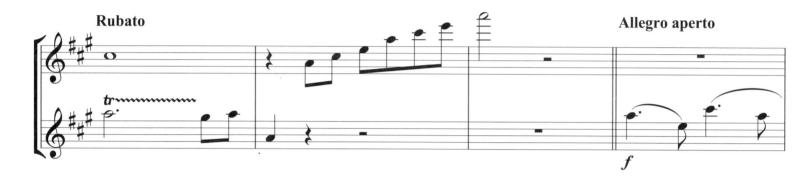

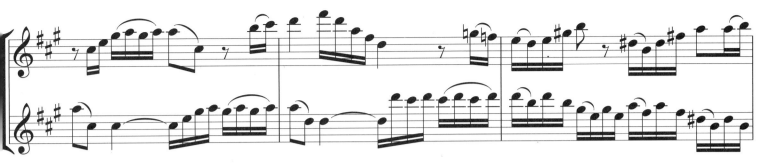

*Violin 2: (Cadenza)*

*Violin 1: (Cadenza)*
*all grace notes gliss wherever possible*

*Violin 2: (Cadenza)*

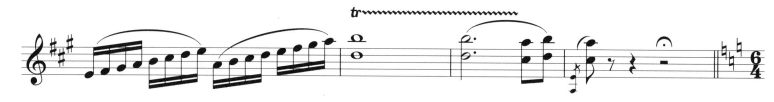

*Violin 1: (Cadenza)*
*leggiero*

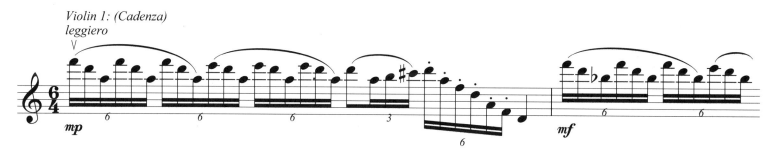

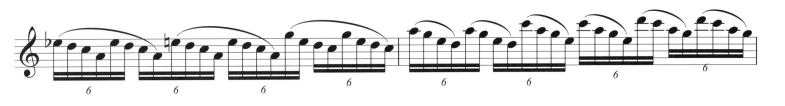

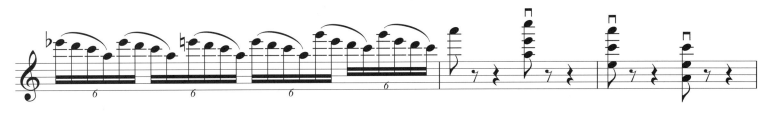

# A LETTER CAME FOR YOU

VIOLIN

By KRIS BOWERS

# IT'S CALLED ERNESTINE

By KRIS BOWERS

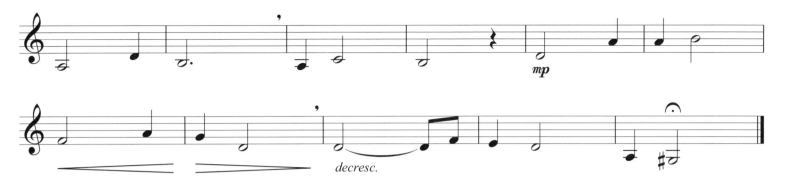

# THE KISS

By KRIS BOWERS

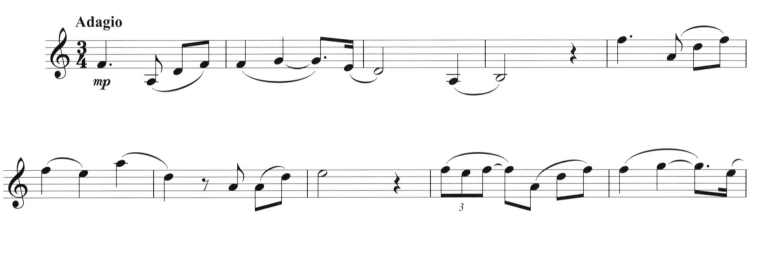

# SOUL OF AN ARTIST

VIOLIN

By MICHAEL ABELS

# WE'LL FIND A DESERT ISLAND

By KRIS BOWERS

# NOT A QUEEN OF FRANCE

VIOLIN

By KRIS BOWERS

# COMPOSING THE FINALE

VIOLIN

By KRIS BOWERS

# THE QUEEN IS HERE - YOU WILL BE ERASED

By KRIS BOWERS

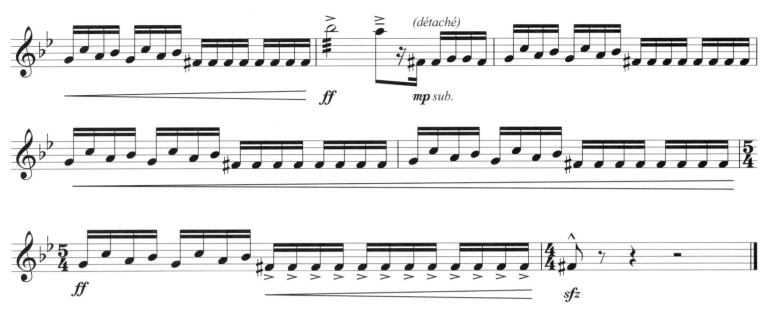

# O CESSATE DI PIAGARMI FROM "IL POMPEO"

Composed by ALESSANDRO SCARLATTI
Libretto by NICOLÒ MINATO
Arranged by MICHAEL ABELS

# THE ONLY HOME I KNEW

VIOLIN

By KRIS BOWERS

# CHOICES COME FROM WITHIN

By KRIS BOWERS